MAKE WAY FOR

BOSTON DUCK TOURS

™

Hillary Holland
and
Terri Maguire

ISBN: 0615964583
ISBN 13: 9780615964584
HollandMaguire

Photo Credits
Stan Grossfeld/Boston Globe/Getty Images
Rob Tringali/Sportschrome/Getty Images
Damian Strohmeyer/Sports Illustrated/ Getty Images
Yoon S. Byun/The Boston Globe/ Getty Images
Brian Babineau/NBAE/Getty Images
David L. Ryan/The Boston Globe/Getty Images

Additional photography by:
Boston Duck Tours
Dreamstime
Hillary Holland
Barbara Macquarrie

THANK YOU

The authors, Hillary Holland and Terri Maguire, would like to give special thanks to these people for their guidance and feedback during the writing of this book.

Terri's mom, Mabel Hinkle, and her mom's husband, Bill Hinkle
Hillary's mom, Liza Holland
Terri's dad, Jack Maguire, and his wife, Linda Maguire
&
Barbara Donlon
Lynne Emerson
Julian Franco
Deb Griffin
Barbara Macquarrie
David Maguire
John Maguire
Karen Maguire
Mark Maguire
Matt Maguire
Tim O'Connor
Linda Phelan
Richard Robbat
Sally White
Peter Yesair

Hillary and Terri would also like to thank family and friends for their love and support.

This book is dedicated to learners everywhere, with special fondness for the students, families, and staff of the Lynch School community, both past and present.

Thanks also goes to Boston Duck Tours' Jim Healy and Bob Schwartz for supporting the project and to Cindy Brown for believing in us and for allowing us this opportunity.

WELCOME TO BOSTON, THE BIRTHPLACE OF AMERICAN LIBERTY

Whether you are fortunate enough to live near this historic city or you are a visitor to the area, Boston offers a wealth of interesting sites to explore.

This city is filled with never-ending learning experiences around every corner. On your ride, America's amazing story will begin to unfold.

You are so lucky to be here! Now sit back, absorb the rich history, and enjoy the journey.

1

A NOTE FROM THE PRESIDENT & CEO OF BOSTON DUCK TOURS

Thank you for your interest in Boston Duck Tours, and welcome to Boston! A Boston Duck Tour is a great introduction to our wonderful city. You can learn about our rich history, famous 'firsts,' and interesting facts about the people and events that have made 'Beantown' the vibrant, fascinating place it is today.

When you finish the tour, I hope you'll go on to explore the different neighborhoods that give Boston its diverse flavor. Boston is known as America's walking city. Set off on foot and spend some time exploring Beacon Hill, with its historic homes and unique boutiques. The small shops and authentic restaurants of the North End are easy to see in an afternoon, and historic Faneuil Hall offers hundreds of shopping and dining opportunities. Stroll along the waterfront and the Charles River Esplanade. Then rest on a bench in our beautiful Public Garden. (In season, you can enjoy a Swan Boat ride.) Take in the stately homes along Commonwealth Avenue, and stop in at the galleries, cafes, and shops of Back Bay and the South End.

I want to thank you for your patronage. I know you'll have a memorable time in Boston, the birthplace of American freedom. All of us here at the Boston Duck Tours hope you will join us again!

Cindy Brown
President & CEO
Boston Duck Tours

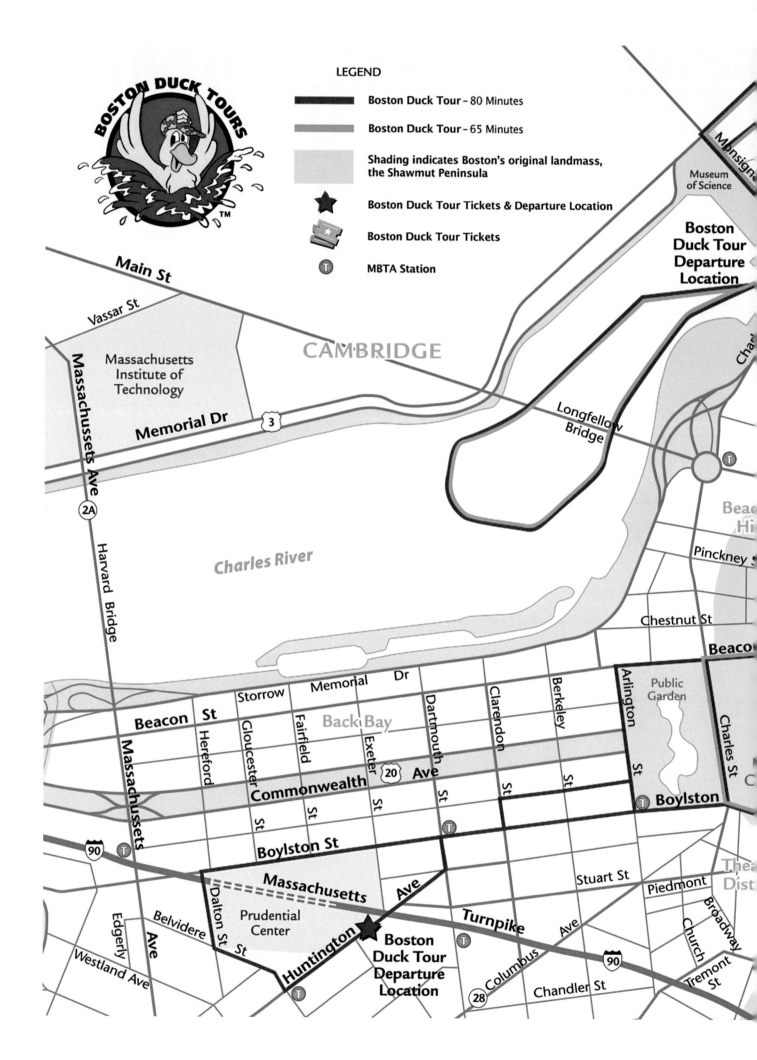

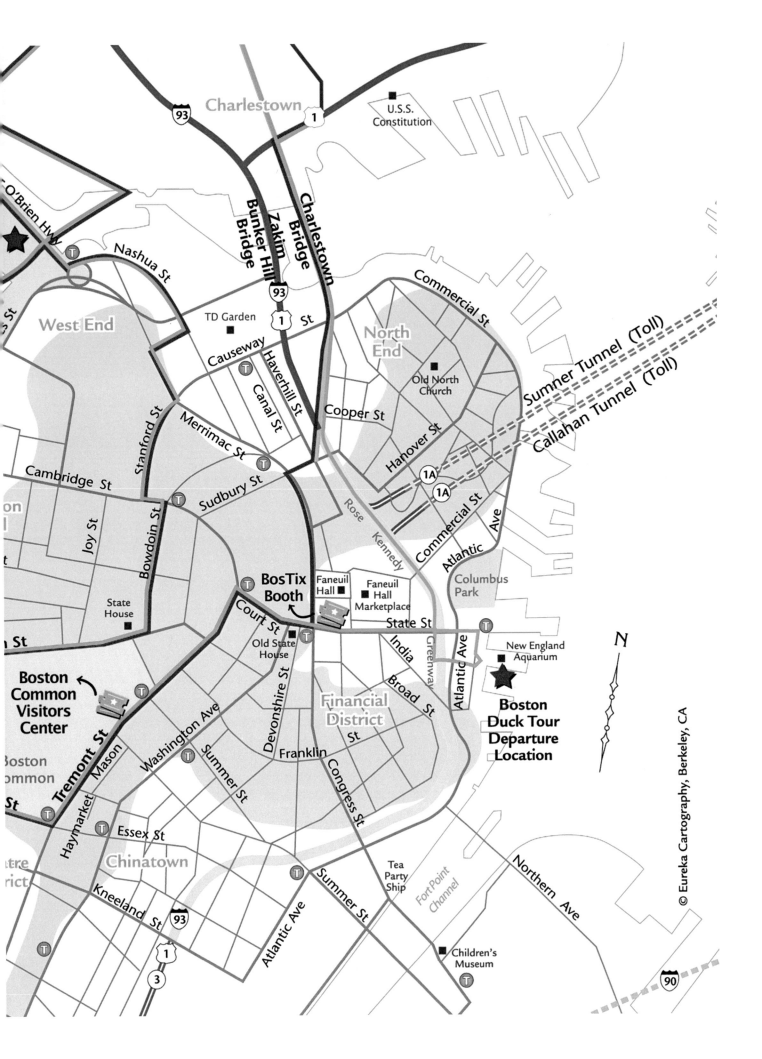

DUCKS

The Duck Tour vehicles, which carry more than six hundred thousand visitors yearly through the winding streets of Boston and into the Charles River, have become a familiar sight around town. As well as having creative names like *Beantown Betty, Faneuil Holly, Old Gloria, Charlie River,* and *Tub of the Hub,* these decorated vehicles are easily recognizable. With elevated, open-air seating and unobstructed views, the Ducks allow riders a unique learning experience whether traveling through the historic streets of Boston or splashing into the Charles River.

The Boston Duck Tour fleet has its own place in history. When the company was founded in 1994, Boston Duck Tours used original World War II DUKWs. During wartime, these amphibious vehicles were built for the United States military to transport troops and cargo, and they played an instrumental role in both European and Pacific theaters. In 1944, during the World War II conflict, the DUKWs carried troops onto the beaches of Normandy in an invasion known as D-Day. An impressive 684 DUKWs were assigned to the invasion. They were used to carry soldiers and supplies from larger vessels in deep water directly onto land. This means of transportation was also used to retrieve wounded soldiers from battle and return them to safety on awaiting ships. Named DUKW by their manufacturer, General Motors, these vehicles were nicknamed Ducks by the soldiers because of their ability to successfully navigate both land and sea.

Once they had been retired by the military, the fleet of twenty-one thousand DUKW vehicles found homes in the United States and around the world. Boston Duck Tours was fortunate to acquire some of the original vehicles for their fleet. Unfortunately, after many years of service, the old World War II DUKWs were worn out, and repair parts became hard to find. Therefore, Boston Duck Tours retired their old DUKWs and are now using modern replicas, which are more efficient, running on biodiesel fuel.

These moving landmarks have been used to carry hometown teams during their championship parades through the crowds of cheering fans lining the streets of Boston. Since their debut parade for the 2002 Super Bowl victory of the New England Patriots, the Ducks have transported all four of Boston's professional sports teams in championship celebrations.

Whether sharing excitement with sports fans or history with visitors, the Ducks offer a joyful experience, bringing smiles to riders and spectators alike along the streets of Boston.

BOSTON COMMON

The Boston Common, America's oldest public park, was founded in 1634. Forty-eight acres of land were purchased by the Puritans from William Blackstone, the first European settler in Boston. For the next two hundred years, this land was common space used by families for raising cattle. By 1830, however, due to overgrazing, cows were banned from the Common. This shared space eventually evolved into Boston's first public park.

This is the site of America's first witch hangings. In 1648, Margaret Jones was accused of being a witch and was hanged from an elm tree on the Common. Surprisingly, this was forty-four years before the famous Salem witch trials took place. This elm tree, known as the Great Elm, was frequently used as a gallows to hang criminals sentenced to death. Hangings took place on the Boston Common until it was officially banned in 1817.

During the British occupation of Boston during the Revolutionary War, the British trained and quartered their soldiers on Boston Common. And it was from here that the Redcoats organized and began their march to Lexington and Concord, where the first shots of the American Revolution were fired.

In more recent years, the Boston Common has been host to many different gatherings. Most notably, in 1965, one hundred thousand people assembled to protest the Vietnam War. Also in 1965, Dr. Martin Luther King Jr. spoke to a crowd of more than twenty thousand people in a rally addressing the city about its racial issues. In 1979, over four hundred thousand people took part in a Mass led by Pope John Paul II as he spoke to the youth of America.

In 1987, the Boston Common was granted its status as a National Historic Landmark. Today, the public enjoys the Boston Common year round. One of the Common's most popular attractions is the manmade Frog Pond. Alive with activity, each season offers unique experiences. During the summer months, the Frog Pond becomes a wading pool and spray fountain, cooling its visitors from the heat of the summer sun. In the cold winter months, the pond is a smooth ice-skating rink where skaters can twirl and glide through the crisp New England air. In the spring and fall, the pond is a reflecting pool, offering a serene setting where visitors may play, relax, read, or gather with friends.

BUNKER HILL MONUMENT

British troops were sent to occupy Boston in 1768. During the ensuing years of occupation, sometimes-violent protests erupted. The colonists, frustrated with British rule and taxation, united as rebels in an attempt to fight back against the forces. Following the Battle of Lexington and Concord, the patriot militia companies surrounded Boston, blocking the British from leaving the city. On June 17, 1775, a momentous battle was fought between British soldiers and New England militia.

The commander of the British forces, General Thomas Gage, devised a plan to break out of the city and disperse the rebels. To do this, the British troops would have to cross the mouth of the Charles River to Charlestown. Through secret intelligence operations, the rebels learned of Britain's plans and moved troops into Charlestown's highest grounds, known today as Bunker Hill and Breed's Hill. These two hills in Charlestown overlooked the harbor and were prime strategic vantage points.

Today, confusion still exists about the names of these two hills. The larger hill is named Bunker Hill, and the smaller is Breed's Hill. The Bunker Hill Monument actually stands on the lower of the two hills, Breed's Hill, where the battle took place. It is believed that the battle and the monument were named for the area's closest known landmark, which was the higher hill, Bunker Hill.

Preparing to defend the higher grounds, militia forces worked to fortify the lower of the two hills. They dug knee-deep trenches and built chest-high fences strengthened by hay and sod to ready the area for attack. Down below, while a fleet of eight British naval ships patrolled the harbor's waters, British soldiers drilled and organized troops on the land known as Boston Common.

On a hot June day, British troops, overheated in traditional woolen uniforms and weakened by poor living conditions and a lack of supplies, marched in line formation up the lower hill to confront the New England militia. The militia, made up of farmers, doctors, lawyers, and shopkeepers, were inexperienced but fought valiantly against what was known to be the greatest and most qualified military force of the time. It is believed that the leader of the rebel forces, Colonel William Prescott, commanded his troops with these famous words: *Don't fire until you see the whites of their eyes.* This instruction meant, in order to save their scarce ammunition, his troops were not to shoot until the British soldiers were close. However, there is no evidence that these words were actually spoken. Some historians believe that Colonel William Prescott commanded his men not to fire until British troops were within thirty yards. Militia forces were also instructed to shoot the best-dressed British soldiers first, knowing these would be the higher-ranking officers.

After two failed attempts to take higher ground and suffering many casualties, including two-thirds of their officers, the demoralized British soldiers regrouped and marched up the hill in their third wave of attack. Out of ammunition, the patriots had to resort to bayonets and hand-to-hand fighting against the better-equipped British. Militia forces eventually retreated, giving up control of this strategic vantage point.

This became the first major battle and the bloodiest encounter of the Revolutionary War, and it showed the colonists that the world's strongest army was not invincible. Although they lost to the British soldiers, colonists gained a psychological victory that was a catalyst for uniting colonial forces.

The Bunker Hill Monument stands on the lower hill as a tribute to all of the patriots who fought in the battle. The monument stands 221 feet tall, and it takes 294 steps to climb to its peak. Work began on its construction in 1825, but frequent work stoppages caused by a lack of funds delayed its completion until 1842. Portions of the funds used for construction of the monument came from the sale of battlefield land as house lots. Boston women also organized additional fundraisers, selling baked goods and handmade crafts to raise money for the monument.

Today the Bunker Hill Monument, a highly visible structure, stands boldly against the Boston skyline as a constant reminder of the brave patriots who fought and died here so that America could be free.

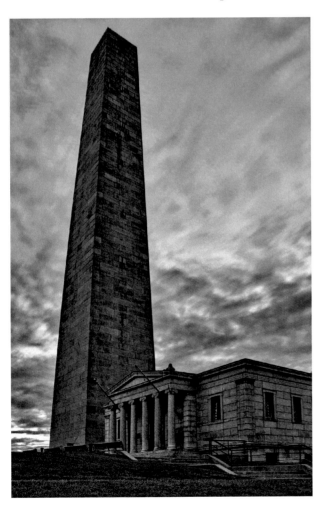

CHARLES RIVER

Carved by glaciers, the Charles River is the longest river in Massachusetts, measuring eighty miles in length. Starting in Hopkinton, it winds its way through twenty-two towns and cities before reaching Boston and its final destination, the Atlantic Ocean. Early settlers originally called it the Massachusetts River after a local Native American tribe. Believing that Native Americans were savages, Young Prince Charles I of England renamed it after himself.

Over its history, the banks of the Charles River became heavily populated with industrial activity. Companies used the river's hydropower to fuel their mills and factories, which created massive pollution. Environmentally, the harm was far-reaching. Sewage, oil, road runoff, urban trash, and factory waste were routinely dumped into the river, causing algae blooms, triggering fish kills, and turning its waters pink and orange. Due to this environmental devastation, the last mile of the Charles River was known as the *lost mile*. Eventually, this once popular river became unsafe for healthy human contact and was considered to be an ecological disaster.

Efforts to clean and restore the ecological balance of the Charles River began in 1995. Today, the river is rated as one of the nation's cleanest, and Boston area residents and visitors use it for recreational activities, including boating, fishing, and bird-watching. Although the river water is clean enough to swim in for most of the year, swimming has not yet been officially added to the list of recreational activities because sediments in the mud, when stirred up, could release dangerous toxic pollutants.

The Charles River has more than ten different species of fish and a varied bird population. The cormorant is a common sight. These black shore birds can be seen diving into the water or drip-drying their wings on natural or manmade perching locations along the river.

Popular spectacles take place yearly on the Charles River. Each Fourth of July, crowds gather to celebrate America's Independence Day in Boston style. On boats on the river and with picnic blankets on its banks, hundreds of thousands of people listen to the Boston Pops Orchestra while watching fireworks explode overhead. In October, the Charles River is host to the world's largest two-day rowing event, the Head of the Charles Regatta. Established in 1965, the race attracts rowers from around the world. Each spring, the Charles River Watershed Association hosts the annual The Run of the Charles Canoe and Kayak Race, kicking off the start of the boating season. Spectators line the banks of the Charles River and crowd its bridges to watch these festivities.

In the water or on its shores, visitors today enjoy the Charles River as its natural, healthy balance thrives.

FANEUIL HALL

Located in downtown Boston, Faneuil Hall is one of the nation's most visited tourist attractions. With more than eighteen million visitors yearly, Faneuil Hall is a lively venue offering both indoor and outdoor shopping and entertainment. The original building, Faneuil Hall, built in 1742, stands in front of the three buildings known as Faneuil Hall Marketplace. Built in 1826, the middle building, Quincy Market, sits between the North Market and the South Market buildings.

Faneuil Hall is one of Boston's oldest public markets. It was donated to the city by a wealthy businessman, Peter Faneuil, as a location for commerce and trade. Offering its patrons a variety of produce and meat was not its only function however. Faneuil Hall's second-floor public meeting space has long been a site for political meetings and debates. The earliest meetings were credited as being the catalyst for change in American history, earning Faneuil Hall its nickname, The Cradle of Liberty.

Standing in front of Faneuil Hall is a statue of Samuel Adams, an influential patriot in the years prior to the Revolutionary War. His speeches and articles opposing English rule inspired and motivated colonists seeking independence. The Revolutionary politics debated in Faneuil Hall sparked significant protests against major issues, such as the Sugar Act, the Stamp Act, and the Tea Act, the latter of which resulted in the legendary Boston Tea Party on December 16, 1773. In the years that followed, rallies continued in this building and helped to spark other protests during the antislavery and women's rights movements.

On top of Faneuil Hall is a brass grasshopper. Popular folklore credits this fifty-two-inch, thirty-eight-pound weathervane as a tool used to expose suspected spies during the War of 1812. The grasshopper was a familiar sight to the citizens of Boston, and it was said therefore any person not able to disclose the shape of the weathervane when questioned was considered a spy! However, there is no historical evidence validating this urban myth.

Faneuil Hall's central cobblestone plaza hosts a variety of street performers, local artisans, specialty kiosks, restaurants, and food vendors. On any given day, Faneuil Hall is a bustling mecca of entertainment and culinary choices, filled with the sights, sounds, and aromas of a thriving center of cultural activity.

FENWAY PARK

Home of the Boston Red Sox, this historic park opened in 1912 and is the oldest Major League Baseball Ballpark in the nation. On game nights the areas in and around the ballpark are alive with excitement. Yawkey Way, the home of Fenway Park, is closed to traffic and open to fans and vendors for pregame festivities. During the game, passionate fans fill the stadium to root for their home team. Their energy is positively electric, creating a magical atmosphere. The bright lights of the intimate, old-time ballpark illuminate the stadium, enveloping the fans in the vibrant greens of the plush grass, the stadium seating, and the Green Monster.

Standing thirty-seven feet two inches high, the Green Monster wall in left field challenges batters with its height and has put a stop to many would-be homeruns. In 1934, the scoreboard was installed in the wall. It is the oldest remaining manually operated scoreboard in Major League Baseball. During games, scorekeepers hidden behind the wall continuously update scores from around the league.

A solo red stadium seat marks the landing spot of the longest homerun ever hit at Fenway Park. In 1946, Boston slugger Ted Williams hit the 502-foot blast that soared from home plate to section 43, row 37, seat 21 and bounced off of an unsuspecting fan's straw hat. This commemorative chair, located behind the bullpen, high among the outfield seats, marks this historic milestone and presents a visual challenge to any player stepping up to bat.

Due to the following of loyal fans, also known as Red Sox Nation, Fenway Park boasts the longest-standing record of consecutive sold-out home games in Major League Baseball history.

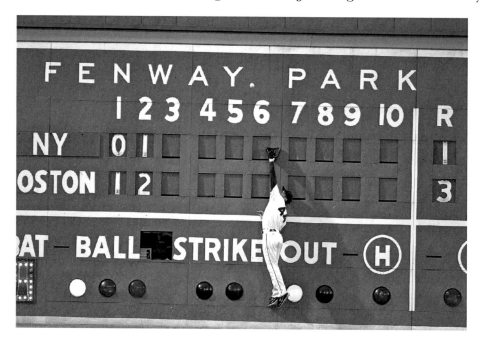

KING'S CHAPEL BURIAL GROUND AND KING'S CHAPEL

King's Chapel Burial Ground is the oldest burying site in Boston. Founded in 1630, this was Boston's sole cemetery for thirty years. The oldest gravesites were marked with wooden headstones, which eventually disintegrated due to New England's harsh weather. Many markers made out of stone are still standing, having survived hundreds of years. The oldest one dates back to 1658. Early tombstones were void of ornamentation, usually displaying only the name and the deceased's dates of birth and death. Later, toward the end of the 1600s, tombstones were engraved with winged skulls, crossbones, and hourglasses, symbolizing death and the expiration of time here on earth.

Among the people buried in the King's Chapel Burial Ground are John Winthrop, the first governor of Massachusetts Bay Colony prior to the Revolutionary War; Mary Chilton, often said to be the first woman to step off the *Mayflower* (however, there is no historical record to validate this claim); and the father and grandfather of William Dawes, famous for his midnight ride with Paul Revere. Although a plaque and a tomb remain labeled in William Dawes's honor, it is believed that Dawes's body lays interned across town in a family burial plot in Boston's Jamaica Plain.

In an effort to establish the Church of England's presence in Boston, King James II's governor seized a portion of the public burial ground after no citizen would willingly sell property to him. On this land in 1688, he built the King's Chapel. In 1754, a larger stone structure was built around the original building. The original wooden structure was dismantled and removed through the windows of the new church.

The King's Chapel tower now houses the last bell made by Paul Revere. After the original bell cracked in 1814, Paul Revere's foundry melted it down, recast it, and rehung the new bell in 1816. Paul Revere said it was the sweetest sounding bell he ever made. Weighing 2,437 pounds, this bell is still rung by hand every Sunday.

NEW ENGLAND HOLOCAUST MEMORIAL

Remember. This single word is carved in the stone walkway welcoming visitors to the Holocaust Memorial. Located near Faneuil Hall, the six structures that make up the memorial stand as a powerful reminder of the mass extermination of Jews and other minorities that occurred during World War II, between the years of 1939 and 1945.

A large block of granite stands on each end of the memorial. One is inscribed with the word *Holocaust,* while written on the other is the word *Shoah,* the Hebrew term for the Holocaust. Visitors often leave small stones atop the granite structures in remembrance of those who died in the Holocaust. A black granite pathway leads guests through each tower of the memorial. Mist drifts upward through metal grates at the base of the towers. Each of the six glass towers, which stand fifty-four feet high, memorializes one million people put to death during the Holocaust. These six chambers are labeled with the names of the six main Nazi death camps where the victims perished.

Covering the glass walls, in neat rows, are six million numbers representing the six million Jewish victims of the Holocaust. Also etched in the glass throughout the monument are historical facts and personal quotes from survivors, family members, and liberating soldiers.

Boston area survivors conceived the idea for the New England Holocaust Memorial, which was dedicated in 1995. The memorial provides a peaceful place to reflect and remember one of history's darkest moments.

OLD GRANARY BURYING GROUND AND PARK STREET CHURCH

The adjacent sites of the Park Street Church and the Old Granary Burial Ground were originally part of the Boston Common. The church, with its 217-foot steeple, was built in 1809 and stands on the location of a former granary, a grain warehouse that was used to store feed for the livestock that Boston's early settlers allowed to graze on the Boston Common.

Established in 1660, the Old Granary Burying Ground is the third oldest of Boston's cemeteries (after King's Chapel and Copp's Hill Burying Ground respectively). More than 2,300 headstones can be seen above ground; however, it is estimated that more than five thousand people lay at rest beneath these markers. Funerals were costly, and frequently one headstone was used to mark an entire family.

Among the people buried in the Old Granary Burying Ground are three signers of the Declaration of Independence, Samuel Adams, John Hancock, and Robert Treat Paine. Another leader of the American Revolution, Paul Revere, is also buried here. These men were members of a group known as the Sons of Liberty and played a key role in motivating and organizing colonists to oppose British occupation and rule. Also buried at this site are the five victims of the Boston Massacre as well as the parents of Benjamin Franklin, an inventor, influential writer, and a prominent political leader during the American Revolution.

The first public performance of the patriotic song "America" was in the Park Street Church on July 4, 1831, sung by the church's children's choir as part of an Independence Day celebration. "America," composed by Samuel Francis Smith, is also known as "My Country, Tis of Thee." For one hundred years, "America" was rivaled in popularity by other patriotic hymns, such as "The Star-Spangled Banner" by Francis Scott Key. In 1931, "The Star-Spangled Banner" was chosen as this country's national anthem.

OLD NORTH CHURCH

Built in 1723, The Old North Church is the oldest church in Boston, and its eight bells are the oldest matched set of bells in any church in America. Located in the North End, the Old North Church is most recognized for its steeple. Standing 191 feet high, this majestic steeple played an important role in helping the colonists as they prepared for battle at the beginning of the American Revolution.

On the night of April 18, 1775, American patriots waited anxiously for a signal alerting them to movement by the British troops. It had been agreed that one lantern would be hung in the steeple of the Old North Church if the British military were seen to be moving over land, and two lanterns would be hung if they traveled by water, the Charles River. Suddenly, light broke through the darkness as two glowing lanterns appeared in the window high up in the steeple of the Old North Church. Illuminated for less than one minute, the lanterns hung just long enough to signal the waiting patriots, without exposing their secret alarm system to the advancing British forces. After receiving the anticipated signal, several riders mounted their horses and set off into the night, house by house, alerting the colonists. Two of the horsemen, William Dawes and Paul Revere, although riding two different routes, had one united goal: reach Lexington in time to warn John Hancock and Samuel Adams, the two leaders of the Sons of Liberty who were facing arrest by the British. The two riders also warned of British troops moving toward Lexington and Concord, where colonists had been secretly stockpiling guns and ammunition.

Although popular belief quotes Paul Revere as shouting, "The British are coming! The British are coming!," these were not the actual words he called into the night, since many of the colonists still considered themselves British. "The Regulars are coming! The Regulars are coming!," is the phrase he proclaimed on that famous night, alerting sleeping citizens as he galloped on horseback through the countryside.

25

OLD STATE HOUSE

The Old State House, built in 1713, is Boston's oldest surviving public building. Located in the heart of the city, it housed Massachusetts's state government until 1798, when the new State House was completed. Constructed in an area bustling with both political and merchant activity, this building was also used as a site of debate over British occupation and rule.

On March 5, 1770, growing tensions and constant altercations between British soldiers and local colonists over British occupation and taxation culminated in a bloody confrontation. This clash ended with British soldiers firing into a crowd of unruly civilians, killing five men and wounding six more. It came to be known as the Boston Massacre. Colonists later used this event as propaganda to unite and strengthen their resolve against a king attempting to maintain control over the colonies from across the ocean. The site is marked by a circle of cobblestones beneath the balcony of the Old State House.

The Declaration of Independence was read to Bostonians from the east balcony of the Old State House on July 18, 1776. This document declared freedom from British rule for the thirteen colonies. The Declaration of Independence is still read from this balcony on the Fourth of July every year.

Two symbols of British monarchy stand atop the roof of the Old State House. The golden crowned lion and the silver unicorn are reminders of America's struggle for independence. These statues are replicas of the originals, which were taken down and ceremoniously burned in a bonfire after Boston's first reading of the Declaration of Independence. On the west side of the Old State House, a statue of an eagle symbolizes the freedom and strength of the united colonies.

Today, the basement of the Old State House is used as a subway station. Another part of the Old State House is a museum operated by the Bostonian Society. This museum houses information about important people and events of the Revolutionary War as well as historical artifacts. Some of the artifacts include: tea from the Boston Tea Party, a red velvet suit worn by John Hancock at his swearing-in as governor, and a cannonball from the Battle of Bunker Hill.

PUBLIC GARDEN

The Public Garden, established in 1837, is America's oldest botanical garden. It is located in the center of Boston, separated from the Boston Common by Charles Street. Once a salt marsh, these twenty-four acres were filled in to become a public garden with winding paths and lush flowerbeds. An assortment of trees, such as weeping willows, elms, and river birch, provide shade in the summertime. Roses and flowering shrubs create a colorful display throughout the growing season. It's the perfect place for enjoying a peaceful stroll in the middle of a bustling city.

America's oldest public garden also contains many manmade attractions. Fountains and statues add to the richness of the park's character, and comfortable benches beckon. Towering above onlookers, a bronze statue of George Washington on horseback, dating from 1869, is a prominent feature in the garden.

The most beloved landmarks in the park are the bronze statues of a mother duck and her eight mallard ducklings. Massachusetts resident Nancy Schon created these statues in 1987. The statues were inspired by the popular children's picture book *Make Way For Ducklings*, written by Robert McCloskey. Another landmark is the suspension bridge, built in 1867, which stretches over the park's four-acre lagoon. This bridge provides walkers with a scenic route above the water, while below, during the warmer months, the Swan Boats glide across the water's surface.

THE ROBERT GOULD SHAW AND MASSACHUSETTS 54TH REGIMENT MEMORIAL

Situated on the Boston Common, across the street from the "new" State House, is the Robert Gould Shaw and Massachusetts 54th Regiment Memorial.

After Massachusetts abolished slavery in 1783, numerous free black slaves set up residence in the Boston neighborhood now known as Beacon Hill. The Civil War broke out in 1861, and after President Lincoln signed the Emancipation Proclamation two years later, many free blacks were eager to join the fight. These brave men knew that the stakes were high. If captured, enslavement or death awaited. But to them, the words in the Declaration of Independence, "All men are created equal," were worth fighting for.

Massachusetts's Governor John Andrew created the first official all-black volunteer Union infantry, the Massachusetts 54th Regiment. Although they were able to fight as enlisted soldiers, black men were not allowed to serve as officers. Therefore, the Massachusetts 54th Regiment was led by twenty-five-year-old Colonel Robert Gould Shaw. A white man of privilege, Shaw was the son of two of Boston's active abolitionists.

The monument represents Colonel Shaw and his troops leaving from the foot of the State House on Beacon Hill, marching south to fight for the Union army. Two short months later, on July 18, 1863, in an attack on Confederate stronghold Fort Wagner in South Carolina, the infantry suffered many casualties, including the death of Colonel Shaw. Although the Battle of Fort Wagner was a physical defeat for the Union, it served as emotional momentum, encouraging an insurgence of black enlistees.

Augustus Saint-Gaudens created this bronze sculpture, and after thirteen years of passionate effort, his work was dedicated in 1897. Originally, Augustus's memorial was that of a solitary Gould Shaw on horseback. However, at the request of Shaw's family, Saint-Gaudens added the black soldiers alongside their leader. In 1982, the names of the sixty-two soldiers that died at the Battle of Fort Wagner with Colonel Robert Gould Shaw were added to the base of the monument.

The Robert Gould Shaw Memorial is the starting point of Boston's Black Heritage Trail. This walking tour introduces visitors to some of Boston's rich diverse history. Visitors will see notable sites along the trail, such as the African Meeting House. This is the oldest black church still standing in the United States, dating back to 1806. Also along the trail is the Lewis and Harriet Hayden House, a safe house for escaped slaves traveling the Underground Railroad. The Haydens, themselves fugitive slaves, were known to have kept two kegs of gunpowder on their porch. When slave hunters came to remove runaway slaves, the Haydens threatened to ignite the gunpowder, preferring to cause a grand explosion and death rather than surrendering the fugitive slaves.

STATE HOUSE

The "new" State House is located on top of Beacon Hill, overlooking the Boston Common. It was built in 1798 on a cow pasture originally owned by John Hancock, the state's first elected governor post-Revolutionary War. This red brick building is home to Massachusetts's state government. Within its walls and on its grounds, this living museum contains many historical artifacts and memorabilia showcasing Massachusetts's role in America's struggle for liberty and freedom.

The State House is easily recognizable by its golden dome, which throughout its history has seen many transformations. Originally it was covered with wooden shingles, which did not weather well. Leaks forced renovations, and in 1802 Paul Revere's company sheathed the dome in rolled copper. In 1874 the copper dome was covered in a paper-thin layer of twenty-three-karat gold leaf. During World War II, yet another transformation took place: the dome was temporarily painted gray-black for camouflage during blackouts to protect the city from nighttime bomber raids.

The wooden pinecone decorating the top of the State House dome symbolizes Massachusetts's rich history in the lumber industry, which dates back to colonial times. It also represents Massachusetts's connection with Maine, which was part of Massachusetts until 1820, when Maine became its own state. While still part of the territory, Maine provided timber used to build the new State House.

Inside the House of Representatives hangs the "Sacred Cod." This five-foot painted wooden codfish, a replica of a fish commonly found in the Atlantic waters off the Massachusetts coast, symbolizes the importance of the fishing industry to people of New England.

The dome measures fifty feet at its diameter and towers fifty feet above the State House floor at its peak. This grand structure is more than just a beautiful sight. It is from the center of the State House dome that all distances to surrounding towns are calculated, truly making the State House the epicenter of Boston.

SWAN BOATS

Since 1877, the Swan Boats have been one of Boston's most popular tourist attractions. Floating serenely in the Swan Boats, on the lagoon in the Public Garden, visitors are pedaled around the pond by the operator sitting inside the body of a swan. Steered by pulleys, rudders, and ropes, each of the six boats can carry twenty passengers seated on benches.

The boats are still owned and operated by the descendants of Robert Paget, the original designer and builder. The design has changed very little over the years. In addition to incorporating the artistic shape of the swan, the family combined the newly popular technology of the bicycle. The inspiration for these charming pleasure vessels was the opera *Lohengrin*, a romantic medieval story in which a swan pulls a boat across a river.

The Swan Boats operate from the end of April through the end of September. While being pedaled quietly across the surface of the lagoon, riders can enjoy the colorful landscape of the Public Garden as well as the beauty of a pair of live swans, which are imported to the pond each year.

TD GARDEN

The TD Garden (formerly known as The Boston Garden) is home to two of Boston's most success-ful professional sports teams, the Celtics and the Bruins. The original Garden was built in 1928 and was one of the smallest professional sports arenas in the country. Throughout the years, the building has hosted other sporting events as well as political rallies, circuses, and concerts. Many rock 'n' roll legends performed within the walls of this intimate venue, including James Brown, KISS, The Who, Bruce Springsteen, the Rolling Stones, the Beatles, and Elvis.

Although well loved, the original Garden had many flaws. With no air conditioning, an under-sized hockey rink, cramped seating, and many seats with obstructed views, the venue eventually be-came obsolete. Construction began on the new Garden in 1993. During the construction of the new building, the original Garden continued to host events. In October of 1995, the new building was completed, and the original Boston Garden was retired. The original Boston Garden was left vacant for more than two years, and it was torn down in 1998. Before demolition only nine inches separated the old and the new arenas.

Not only did the original Garden have a rich sporting history, but it was said to be haunted. On oc-casion, players and spectators reported seeing movement and shadows high up among the champion-ship flags. Objects were said to disappear from locker rooms, giving credence to this folklore. During the demolition of the Garden, the remains of a capuchin monkey were found in the rafters, perhaps solving this mystery. It is believed that this escaped circus performer, nicknamed the Boston Monkey, lived in the Garden for an unknown number of years, surviving on discarded concession snacks. Never winning any championships or titles of his own, this Boston Monkey still became a legend.

USS CONSTITUTION

Built in Boston at the Hartt's shipyard, the USS *Constitution* is the oldest commissioned naval vessel afloat. This American treasure is a symbol of strength and freedom. First launched in 1797, with a crew of over 450 men, its original mission was to provide protection for American merchant ships against pirates in the Mediterranean Sea. Whether defending American interests against pirates or against Great Britain, the world's strongest naval force of the time, the USS *Constitution* won all of its battles and boasts the title of "history's greatest ship."

The USS *Constitution* was built for speed. The frigate's thirty-six sails are held by three masts, the tallest being 220 feet. When unfurled, the sails harnessed the power of the wind and propelled the ship's sleek hull across the ocean. This 1,575-ton vessel measures 204 feet in length and 43.5 feet in width and, in its prime, could out-sail smaller British frigates.

Not only was the USS *Constitution* a speedy boat, but it was also very sturdy. It was built from live oak, known to be some of the strongest timber in North America. This frigate's physical structure was designed with military strength. Additional fortification was used throughout the frame of the ship to support the weight of the forty-four cannons on board. Where rival ships used eighteen-pound balls, this United States vessel used twenty-four-and thirty-two-pounders. Having more cannons and larger cannon balls than any other ship of its time, the USS *Constitution* was a well-armed warrior.

The USS *Constitution* was given its name by America's first president, George Washington. Its nickname, Old Ironsides, was earned during the War of 1812 in a battle with Great Britain's ship the *Guerriere*. An eighteen-pound British cannonball was said to have been unable to penetrate the ship and bounced off the USS *Constitution*'s hull without leaving a mark. At that time a sailor reportedly yelled, "Huzzah, her sides are made of iron!"

On many occasions throughout the years, the public has come to Old Ironsides's aide. Two notable campaigns involved America's youth. In 1925, children of America participated in the Pennies Campaign and raised money to restore the vessel and keep it from the scrap heap. In 1997 the money collected by schoolchildren was used to purchase sails for the USS *Constitution*'s two-hundredth-year anniversary sail.

Every year on July 4, in celebration of Independence Day, the USS *Constitution* is tugged into the waters of Boston Harbor. Other cruises also take place on five or six occasions throughout the year, including its yearly turnaround, ensuring that the exterior of this grand ship weathers evenly while tethered to the dock.

The USS *Constitution* has sailed under her own power only twice in the past one hundred years. Sails unfurled, this vessel cruised the ocean waters unaided in 1997 and 2012.

Twice daily, at 8:00 a.m. and at sunset, as the flag of the United States is raised and lowered, a cannon is fired from Old Ironsides.

ABOUT THE AUTHORS

Hillary Holland

Born and raised in a suburb of Boston, Hillary attended the Lynch Elementary School in Winchester, Massachusetts. Hillary received her undergraduate degree from the University of Massachusetts, Amherst, and her master's degree at Merrimack College. While at Merrimack, fond memories of her first grade experience brought her back to the Lynch School, where she was a student teacher with her former first grade teacher, Terri Maguire. Hillary has been fortunate to be able to start her teaching career at the Lynch Elementary School. As an avid traveler, Hillary has visited five continents. Her favorite excursions include a South African great white shark cage dive, hiking a volcano in Guatemala, and exploring Buddhist temples in Thailand.

Terri Maguire

Terri was born and raised in a suburb of Boston. After receiving her undergraduate degree from Boston College and earning a master's degree with Cambridge College, Terri began her teaching career at the Lynch Elementary School in Winchester, Massachusetts, where she has been ever since. In the year 2000, Terri was honored to have been a semifinalist for Massachusetts Teacher of the Year. Her classroom houses a zoo filled with a variety of creatures, including a very large, free-roaming, diaper-wearing sulcata tortoise. Terri shares her love of life and the environment by engaging her students in rich, hands-on experiences. Bringing the curriculum to life, Terri expands her classroom by taking her students on as many as six field trips yearly. Student favorites include howling with live wolves, reconstructing a pilot whale skeleton, and exploring tide pools.

Along with a professional relationship, a friendship quickly developed between the two educators. Together, Terri and Hillary's adventures have included skydiving, hot air ballooning, along with exploring the streets of Boston while researching this book. Passionate about Boston, Terri and Hillary are excited to share its rich history with readers, both young and old alike. With one novice and one well seasoned, both are impassioned teachers and lifelong learners.

Made in the USA
Middletown, DE
13 June 2015